Newness

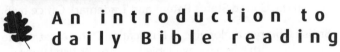

An introduction to
daily Bible reading

John Eddison

Newness of Life: An introduction to daily Bible reading
Copyright © 2011 John Eddison

Published by 10Publishing, a division of 10ofthose.com

Unit 19 Common Bank Industrial Estate
Ackhurst Road
Chorley
PR7 1NH

Email: info@10ofthose.com
Website: www.10ofthose.com

British Library Cataloguing in Publication Data. A catalogue record for this book is available from the British Library

ISBN: 9781906173128

Design & Print Management by: www.printbridge.co.uk

The Way Ahead

NORMAN WARREN

CONTACT PASTOR GEOFF WILL...
01772-752205
KINGS CHURCH, COP LANE
PENWORTHAM
SUNDAYS 10.30 & 6pm

A PRACTICAL GUIDE TO CHRISTIAN LIVING

How can I be sure?

Am I a Christian?
I don't feel a Christian
How can I know I am a Christian?
How can I be sure I am a Christian?

Most Christians at some time ask themselves these questions. Often they become real doubts that cause a lot of unnecessary worry and unhappiness. Possibly you are asking yourself these same questions now.

You may have been baptised and confirmed; you may have gone to church for years—yet you cannot say definitely that you know you are a Christian. You long to be quite sure that your sins are forgiven and that you have eternal life and will go to heaven when you die.

You want to be absolutely certain that Jesus Christ has come into your life and is a living, personal friend. You have opened the door of your life and asked him to come in. You have accepted him. Has he accepted you? How can you be sure? You can be sure because of three things:

- The Bible
- The Cross
- The Holy Spirit

THE BIBLE
How do I know God loves me?
How do I know I have eternal life?
How do I know Jesus rose from the dead and is a living, personal friend, who will be with me moment by moment in my daily life?

Because God says so in the Bible. The Bible is full of the promises of God to all who trust in Jesus Christ. It shows you how to become a Christian; it shows you the way ahead.

The trouble with many Christians is that they do not read the Bible to find out these promises. Instead of relying on them, far too many Christians rely on their own feelings or ideas.

If you are tired or ill, if you have troubles and worries at home or at work, you may not *feel* you are a Christian. Don't rely on your feelings, which change. Trust the promises of God.

Hudson Taylor, the famous missionary to China, once said, 'There is a living God; he has spoken in the Bible. He means what he says and will do all he has promised.'

What does this mean in practice?

How do I know God loves me?
Jesus said, 'God so loved the world that he gave his only Son, that whoever believes in him should not perish but have eternal life.' (John 3:16)

God showed his love for you because he sent Jesus Christ to die on the cross to save you from your sins.

How can I know Jesus is in my life?
Jesus said, 'If any one hears my voice and opens the door, I will come in . . .' (Revelation 3:20)

Have you asked him into your life? Then what does he promise? Clearly and definitely: 'I will come in.'

Don't rely on what you feel; you may not feel any different. If you have asked him in, you can know he has come in, because he says so.

How can I be certain I have eternal life?

Jesus says, 'He who believes has eternal life' (John 6 : 47).

Do you believe in Jesus? Do you trust him? Well then, what does he promise you? Eternal life here and now. You *know* you have eternal life because he promises it to you.

How can I be sure he is with me, if I don't feel him or see him?

Jesus said, 'I am with you always, to the close of the age' (Matthew 28 : 20).

He is with you all the time because he says he will be. Don't rely on what you feel. Trust his promise: 'I am with you always.'

THE CROSS

How do I know God has accepted me and forgiven me all my sins?

One of the results of sin is to cut us off from God. This is why he seems distant and unreal and not concerned with the frustrations and worries of human beings.

The trouble with many Christians is that they go on thinking they can bridge this gap by their own efforts. They think they can win favour with God by being kind,

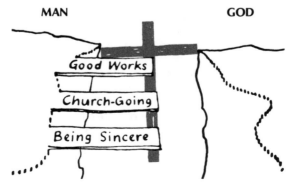

sincere, and honest, and by going to church. They trust their own goodness and good works, hoping they are doing enough to satisfy God. But of course, they can never be sure if they have ever done enough, because they know deep down they are still sinful.

The cross tells you that God accepts you as you are, because, and only because, of what Jesus has done, and not for anything you can ever do.

You can never get through to God on your own. The cross alone bridges the gap between you and God, for Jesus suffered on the cross for your sins to bring you to God (1 Peter 3 : 18). The way back to God is wide open to all who stop trusting in their own goodness and who put their whole trust in Jesus Christ.

The cross tells you that if you trust in Jesus Christ, God will forgive you all your sins. So great was his love for you, that he sent Jesus Christ to save you from the punishment your sin deserves.

Jesus did this by taking the full punishment himself. That is why he cried from the cross, 'My God, my God, why hast thou forsaken me?' (Matthew 27 : 46). For your sake he experienced the awful barrier of sin between man and God. He was cut off from his Father by your sins. Just before he died, Jesus said in a loud voice, 'It is finished!' (John 19 : 30). This was a cry of victory: 'I've done it! The debt of man's sin is paid.'

The trouble with many Christians is that they think they can earn forgiveness by their own efforts. But this is impossible. The Bible says that all our good works are like filthy rags compared to the absolute perfection of God. But there is one way of forgiveness.

The cross tells you that the enormous debt of your sin has been fully paid by Jesus Christ once and for all. Nothing you could ever do could pay this debt.

When you accept Jesus into your heart and life you receive God's forgiveness. Every sin you have ever done is blotted out. God promises not only to forgive all your sin but to forget it as well.

Growing as a Christian

BIBLE READING
Why read the Bible?

The Bible is food
If a baby is to grow properly it must have the right food. If you are to grow strong in the Christian life you also need the right kind of food. God in his love and wisdom has given us this food in the Bible. Your knowledge of him will grow as you find out more about him. Your friendship with Jesus Christ will deepen as you spend time listening when he speaks to you. Your faith in him will grow stronger as you discover more of his power and love.

The Bible is light
To drive a car at night without headlights would be asking for trouble. To try and live the Christian life without reading and knowing and obeying the Bible is equally foolish and dangerous.

Without the Bible we would know very little, if anything, about God or Jesus Christ. We would have no idea where we came from, why we are here, or where we are going. The Bible sheds light on every kind of problem. It speaks with authority on the future, on death, on eternal life, on heaven—to name just a few things. It tells you how you should live your daily life and what God expects of you.

sincere, and honest, and by going to church. They trust their own goodness and good works, hoping they are doing enough to satisfy God. But of course, they can never be sure if they have ever done enough, because they know deep down they are still sinful.

The cross tells you that God accepts you as you are, because, and only because, of what Jesus has done, and not for anything you can ever do.

You can never get through to God on your own. The cross alone bridges the gap between you and God, for Jesus suffered on the cross for your sins to bring you to God (1 Peter 3 : 18). The way back to God is wide open to all who stop trusting in their own goodness and who put their whole trust in Jesus Christ.

The cross tells you that if you trust in Jesus Christ, God will forgive you all your sins. So great was his love for you, that he sent Jesus Christ to save you from the punishment your sin deserves.

Jesus did this by taking the full punishment himself. That is why he cried from the cross, 'My God, my God, why hast thou forsaken me?' (Matthew 27 : 46). For your sake he experienced the awful barrier of sin between man and God. He was cut off from his Father by your sins. Just before he died, Jesus said in a loud voice, 'It is finished!' (John 19 : 30). This was a cry of victory: 'I've done it! The debt of man's sin is paid.'

The trouble with many Christians is that they think they can earn forgiveness by their own efforts. But this is impossible. The Bible says that all our good works are like filthy rags compared to the absolute perfection of God. But there is one way of forgiveness.

The cross tells you that the enormous debt of your sin has been fully paid by Jesus Christ once and for all. Nothing you could ever do could pay this debt.

When you accept Jesus into your heart and life you receive God's forgiveness. Every sin you have ever done is blotted out. God promises not only to forgive all your sin but to forget it as well.

THE HOLY SPIRIT

We have seen that you must not rely on your feelings or your own goodness or your own good works.

You are to rely on:

- What Jesus promises you in the Bible *and*
- What Jesus did for you on the cross.

Is there no place for my feelings?

Yes, there is. When you receive Jesus into your life he gives you the gift of the Holy Spirit. Now the Holy Spirit has two main tasks:

He assures you that you are a Christian

He brings the quiet, yet certain conviction that you are a child of God. You seem to know and feel deep down that you are right with God. Jesus Christ has become a living person to you. The old barrier between you and God is no longer there.

He helps you grow like Jesus

He changes your nature from being self-centred to being Christ-centred. He gives you the power to become gradually more like Jesus himself. This is the work or 'fruit' of the Holy Spirit—to produce in the Christian a nature of love, joy, peace, patience, kindness, goodness, faithfulness, gentleness, self-control. In your own strength you cannot produce this fruit in your life, however hard you try. The Holy Spirit's special work is to give you the inner power to produce this fruit.

What happens if I sin?

When you ask Jesus Christ into your life you become a son or daughter of God. You have begun a new life. You have been born again. Just as you were born into a human family, so, by trusting in Jesus, you are born into God's family:

'. . . as many as received him, to them gave he the right to become the children of God.' (John 1:12 RV) He becomes your Father; you become his child. There is a relationship between you which can never be undone. This does not mean you become perfect overnight.

Well then, what happens if I sin?

A boy, playing cricket in the garden, smashes a window. He had been told not to play there. He keeps out of the way. At mealtime there is an icy silence, for he has disobeyed his father. This lasts until he owns up and says he is sorry. The relationship has not changed; he is still a son. His father could disown him, but he never ceases to be his son. It is the friendship that is broken, until the boy says he is sorry.

When you disobey Christ, or are thoughtless or lazy, when you do, say, or think something you know to be wrong, you are still a child of God; the relationship has not changed, you do not have to ask Jesus Christ into your life again. You have spoiled your friendship with him and it is up to you to say sorry.

Listen to what the Bible says:

'If we say we have no sin, we deceive ourselves, and the truth is not in us. If we confess our sins [i.e. say we are sorry], he [God] is faithful and just, and will forgive our sins and cleanse us from all unrighteousness.' (1 John 1:9)

Growing as a Christian

BIBLE READING
Why read the Bible?

The Bible is food
If a baby is to grow properly it must have the right food. If you are to grow strong in the Christian life you also need the right kind of food. God in his love and wisdom has given us this food in the Bible. Your knowledge of him will grow as you find out more about him. Your friendship with Jesus Christ will deepen as you spend time listening when he speaks to you. Your faith in him will grow stronger as you discover more of his power and love.

The Bible is light
To drive a car at night without headlights would be asking for trouble. To try and live the Christian life without reading and knowing and obeying the Bible is equally foolish and dangerous.

Without the Bible we would know very little, if anything, about God or Jesus Christ. We would have no idea where we came from, why we are here, or where we are going. The Bible sheds light on every kind of problem. It speaks with authority on the future, on death, on eternal life, on heaven—to name just a few things. It tells you how you should live your daily life and what God expects of you.

The Bible is a mirror
You cannot hide things from a mirror. It shows what you are like. If you have a dirty mark on your face the mirror will show it and you can then do something about it.

The Bible will show you what you are really like. It will expose any sin or pride, selfishness or greed. It will show you what you *should* be like and what you *can* be with Christ's help.

When the Bible shows you your faults, do something about it. Repent or turn from them; ask God's forgiveness; determine to be victorious in Christ's strength.

The Bible is a weapon
The Word of God is living and active, sharper than any two-edged sword (Hebrews 4:12). The Bible is the weapon God has given us to defeat the devil. Jesus himself used it when attacked. You too need to get to know it and learn how to use it. With it you will defeat all the devil's cunning attacks, all his temptations for you to doubt Christ or take it easy in the Christian life. With it you will conquer all your fears, all false teaching, all superstitions, all the wrong ideas about Jesus Christ which are so common today.

Reading the Bible

How

The Bible is not an easy book. You need help and you need method. It is not a good idea to start at Genesis and work through the Bible. You will very soon get bogged down and discouraged among all the laws in Leviticus. Nor is it a good idea simply to open the Bible anywhere and hope for the best.

By far the best method is to subscribe to a series of Bible reading aids, such as Scripture Union notes. There are a variety of little booklets available for all ages. You cover the whole Bible in five years. Each day you have ten to fifteen verses, with short notes to help you understand the passage. To give variety, you study first a New Testament book, then one from the Old Testament. Ask your vicar or minister to tell you about them.

When and where

Set aside a definite time when you can be alone and quiet. Most Christians find that early in the morning is the best time, before the rush of the day begins. Others prefer the evening after they have had their meal. Last thing at night is no good if you are too tired to concentrate.

You will only grow as a Christian if you make time to meet with the Lord Jesus and read his Word daily. There are no short cuts to success in the Christian life.

It is very helpful to meet with a group of other Christians and study a passage together.

How to begin
Pray

In your own wisdom you will never understand or enjoy the Bible. Ask the Holy Spirit to help you understand what you read. Use a prayer such as this: 'Open my eyes, that I may behold wondrous things out of thy law' (Psalm 119:18). Now believe that Christ is going to speak to you.

Read slowly

When you have read the passage twice, ask yourself such questions as: 'What do I learn about God?—about Jesus?—about the Holy Spirit?—about man?'

Look for a *promise* to claim, an *example* to follow, a *warning* to heed, a *command* to obey.

Pick out a verse or phrase that has struck you, and learn it, so that you can take this with you into the day.

Memorise

Your memory is certainly not as bad as you probably think it is. One of the greatest helps to growing strong as a Christian is to learn verses of the Bible by heart. Determine to learn one verse every week.

Write the verse out on a card, and on the back of the card put the book, chapter, and verse. Keep these verses with you; go over them again and again. Test yourself in the bus or train. Here are some verses to start: Romans 3:23, Romans 6:23, Isaiah 53:6, Revelation 3:20, Matthew 28:20, John 3:16, John 6:37, 1 John 1:9, 1 Corinthians 10:13.

PRAYER
What is prayer?

When you read the Bible, Christ speaks to you. When you pray, you speak to him. The Christian life is a two-sided friendship.

Prayer is speaking to Jesus Christ about anything, anywhere. It is to the Christian what breathing is to the human body.

Prayer is your direct link with headquarters. When the pocket intercom is switched on, every word is heard by headquarters, who keep a constant listening

watch. Prayer links you directly with your leader—Jesus Christ. Advice, help, and guidance are constantly available to you.

Why pray?

Many people cannot see the point of praying. They say that God knows everything and will work whether they pray or not. We have seen already that by praying we deepen our friendship with Christ. Apart from this a Christian should pray because:

Jesus prayed   If he needed to pray, how much more do you, his follower?

Jesus tells you to pray   As his soldier your aim is to obey him.

Jesus promises to answer prayer   Every prayer will be answered. Sometimes however, his answer will be 'No' or 'Wait'.

It is a sin not to pray   Look up 1 Samuel 12:23.

1 Confess my sins
2 Thank Him for—
3 Pray for others
4 Pray for myself

How to pray
Prayer should follow on naturally from your reading of
the Bible. The early morning is by far the best time for
this. Begin the day with your Friend and Master before
all its rush is upon you.

Try to find a quiet place—maybe your bedroom, or a
front room, or even the kitchen in winter. Try to be
alone if at all possible.

The devil will do everything to stop you praying.
Someone will call or the baby will start to yell. Whatever
happens be determined to guard jealously your quiet
time with the Lord Jesus Christ.

Before you begin to pray, remember quietly to whom
you are coming.

Prayer can take many different forms. Here is one:

Confess your sins　　Man always comes to God as a
sinner needing forgiveness. Ask him to show you your
sins and failings. Ask him to forgive you and to help
you conquer them in the future.

Thank him　　Quietly stop and think of all that you have
to thank him for: the Lord Jesus, the cross, the Bible,
the Holy Spirit, the Church, Christian friends, your
health, your family, answered prayer.

Pray for others　　Get a small notebook and make a list
of people to pray for: your family, friends, leaders in
the State, leaders in your Church, missionaries. Pray
for a few each day. Be definite in your praying, and
don't just make vague requests for God's blessing. As
you pray, use your imagination.

Pray for yourself　　Pray about every aspect of your life:
the day ahead, any problems, duties, or fears, your
witness at home and at work, God's will for your future.

GOING TO CHURCH
What is the Church?
Certainly not just a building. The Bible describes the Church as a family in which we are all brothers and sisters, bound together by love for Christ and for each other. It also describes the Church as a body, Jesus being the head and we being members each with his own job to do. We belong to Jesus and we belong to each other. We need him and we need each other.

There is a great world-wide Church consisting of all who trust in Jesus Christ, whatever their colour, background, or intellect. There are also local churches, parts of the One Church: some Church of England, some Free Church (e.g. Methodist, Baptist).

To be a Christian means to belong to a local church and to support it loyally.

Can I be a good Christian if I do not go to church?
This is as ridiculous as saying, 'I can be a good footballer without joining a team.' A footballer is one who plays in a team. He spends time training with the rest of the team, learning more about the game from them, and

especially from the team coach. Football is a team game. It is the same for the Christian. You cannot call yourself a Christian if you stay at home and do not go to church regularly. It is a different matter of course for very old or sick people who *cannot* get to church.

Why go to church?

If you are a Christian, you go to church:

● To praise and thank God for all his love and goodness to you
● To show openly that you belong to Christ; going to church marks you out as a disciple of Christ
● To meet with other Christians to pray together
● To learn more about the Christian life and to receive strength and guidance for the coming week

If a piece of coal drops from the fire on to the hearth it very soon goes cold and dead. If you stay away from church and Christian fellowship, your love for Christ will very soon go cold and dead. You will lose interest

in reading the Bible and praying. You will lose any desire to win other people for Christ. Your faith will slowly die. Never miss being with Christians in church on Sunday. If there is a weekly Bible-study in your church, make it top priority in your week's activities.

ACTIVE SERVICE

Every Christian is saved to serve. You are now the disciple and servant of Christ. Your one aim in life is to serve and please him.

Here are some of the ways in which you can serve him:

At home

The home is not an easy place to be a Christian, because your family really know you. Show the difference Christ has made to your life by being helpful, thoughtful, patient and, above all, loving.

At work

People at work will watch you to see if your life backs up what you say. Be thorough and efficient in your work, and honest in all your dealings; keep calm when your faith is attacked or laughed at; be ready to speak out at injustices; and be ready to show what Christ means to you personally when opportunity comes.

You should be not only a church member, but also a church worker. You can serve Christ in your local church by cleaning the church, doing the gardening, delivering magazines, singing in the choir. There are other important jobs such as teaching in the Sunday school, or Bible class, helping in a youth club, or visiting in the parish.

Be an active Christian, one who can be trusted.

But the greatest job of all is winning others for Christ. This requires a real love for Christ and a real love for people. It will mean praying for them, befriending them, getting to know them, sharing their interest, talking naturally about Christ, taking them to hear the gospel, or lending them a book or booklet on the Christian life.

The way ahead will not be easy, but you are not alone: Jesus Christ comes with you all the way.

Copyright © N. L. Warren 1966, 1976   *Illustrations* Elizabeth Marsh
First published 1966   *Second edition* 1976   *ISBN* 0 85491 145 6
Printed in Great Britain for
KINGSWAY PUBLICATIONS LTD
1 St Anne's Road, Eastbourne, E. Sussex BN21 3UN by
Stanley L. Hunt (Printers) Ltd, Rushden, Northants

A Falcon Booklet
Kingsway Publications **CPAS**   Price 50p

CONTENTS

Pages

Introduction. 1

(1)   Abide With Me. 2

(2)   Man of Sorrows 4

(3)   Prince of Glory 6

(4)   He is Risen 8

(5)   The Servant King. 10

(6)   The Gift of God. 12

(7)   A New Creation 14

(8)   Take Up the Cross 16

(9)   The Cost of Living 18

(10) A Royal Invitation 20

(11) Springs of Joy. 22

(12) The Way to Win 24

(13) We Shall Overcome 26

(14) The Armour of Light. 28

(15) Walking in the Light 30

(16) The School of Prayer 32

(17) Under New Management. 34

(18) Newness of Life 36

(19) On His Majesty's Service 38

(20) Neighbours!. 40

(21) The King of Love 42

(22) Faith Under Fire 44

(23) The Slough of Despond. 46

(24) Renewal 48

(25) More Than Conquerors. 50

(26) Experience Will Decide. 52

(27) Sober Confidence 54

(28) Unfailing Resources 56

(29) An Experienced Christian 58

(30) Into Battle 60

INTRODUCTION

NEWNESS OF LIFE was first produced over fifty years ago, and it has been widely used and greatly valued ever since. Michael Green in his Foreword to the 1994 edition wrote, "'I must have used it for thirty years in one or other of its editions. I know of no introductory series of Bible reading notes which is as valuable as this".

The purpose of this booklet is primarily to introduce people to the habit of daily Bible reading, and it is hoped that after using it for a month, the reader will adopt one of the many daily Bible reading systems available.[1]

Passages from the Bible have been carefully chosen with people in mind who may quite recently have made a start in the Christian life, and are anxious to understand more about some of the basic truths of the Christian faith.

There are perhaps three things that make the Bible unique amongst books, and its study by the Christian so important. The first is its **Author**, for it claims that while it was written by a wide variety of people, they were each guided and inspired by the Holy Spirit of God. Just as we can speak of St Paul's Cathedral as being 'Christopher Wren's Cathedral', because although he may never have handled a single stone in the construction, it was he who inspired those who did; so we speak of the Bible as 'God's Word' – the principal way in which He has revealed Himself, and spoken to the hearts, minds and consciences of men and women down the ages.

There is next the **Appeal** of the Bible, for it is still the most popular Book in the world, and has been translated into more languages than any other. It owes this appeal to the fact that it contains the answers to all the deepest human needs; and it is to this Book, as to nowhere else, that people have turned to find forgiveness, encouragement, hope and peace of mind. Its appeal is universal, and people of every class and colour, age and ability, have found comfort in its pages.

Finally, the Bible has a very special **Aim**. Most books have some sort of aim – to amuse, inform, excite; but the aim of the Bible is unique, for as we read it, it will throw a remarkable light on human nature; and upon man – 'The glory and the scandal of the universe'; and it will unfold the wisdom and the power, the holiness and the love of God as revealed to us in Jesus Christ.

---

1 For more information regarding the schemes available please contact www.10ofthose.com or sales@10ofthose.com.

(1) Abide With Me

¹³Now that same day two of them were going to a village called Emmaus...
¹⁴They were talking with each other about everything that had happened.
¹⁵As they talked and discussed these things with each other, Jesus
Himself came up and walked along with them; ¹⁶but they were kept from
recognizing Him.

¹⁷He asked them, "What are you discussing together as you walk along?"
They stood still, their faces downcast. ¹⁸One of them, named Cleopas,
asked him, "Are you only a visitor to Jerusalem and do not know the things
that have happened there in these days?"

¹⁹"What things?" he asked.

"About Jesus of Nazareth," they replied... ²⁰"The chief priests and our rulers
handed him over to be sentenced to death, and they crucified him; ²¹but
we had hoped that he was the one who was going to redeem Israel. And
what is more,... some of our women amazed us. They went to the tomb
early this morning ²³but didn't find his body. They came and told us that
they had seen a vision of angels, who said he was alive. ²⁴Then some of our
companions went to the tomb and found it just as the women had said, but
him they did not see."

²⁵He said to them, "How foolish you are, and how slow of heart to believe
all that the prophets have spoken! ²⁶Did not the Christ have to suffer
these things and then enter his glory?" ²⁷And beginning with Moses and
all the Prophets, he explained to them what was said in all the Scriptures
concerning himself.

²⁸As they approached the village to which they were going, Jesus acted as if
he were going farther. ²⁹But they urged him strongly, "Stay with us, for it is
nearly evening; the day is almost over." So he went in to stay with them.

³⁰When he was at the table with them, he took bread, gave thanks, broke
it and began to give it to them. ³¹Then their eyes were opened and they
recognized him, and he disappeared from their sight. ³²They asked each
other, "Were not our hearts burning within us while he talked with us on
the road and opened the Scriptures to us?"

Luke 24:13-32

This familiar story makes a very suitable reading with which to start. First it takes us to the source of Christianity, for our faith does not rest upon 'cleverly invented stories', but upon the historical facts of the birth, life, death, resurrection and ascension of Jesus Christ; and this chapter is one of many accounts of his victory over sin and death by those who were 'eye-witnesses of his majesty' (2 Peter 1:16).

Second, it defines the Christian life for us in the simplest terms. A Christian is not just someone who keeps a lot of rules or performs certain rites. He is someone who has found, as Cleopas and his companion found, that Jesus Christ is not only a figure of history, but a present reality whose friendship can be a living experience.

*Think of the excuses they might have made not to invite Jesus home. Perhaps the house was in a mess, the spare room unswept and the bed unaired: Too **bad** for Jesus! Or perhaps they had a lot to do and next week's work to prepare for: Too **busy** for Jesus! With a quiet 'Good night', Jesus would have continued his journey, and they would have missed the most wonderful experience. But they made no such shallow excuses. Instead they gave that immortal invitation which has been woven into one of our most famous hymns, 'Abide with me, fast falls the eventide'.*

Thought: We can never be 'too bad' to invite Jesus into our lives, but we may easily think we are 'too busy' to do so.

Prayer

O Lord, I need Your presence every passing hour. I need Your forgiveness for my sins, Your power to conquer temptation, and Your wisdom to guide me. Abide with me, now and forever. **Amen**

(2) Man of Sorrows

27Then the governor's soldiers took Jesus... 29and... twisted together a crown of thorns and set it on his head. They put a staff in his right hand and knelt in front of him and mocked him. "Hail, king of the Jews!" they said. 30They spit on him, and took the staff and struck him on the head again and again. 31After they had mocked him, they took off the robe and put his own clothes on him. Then they led him away to crucify him.

32As they were going out, they met a man from Cyrene, named Simon, and they forced him to carry the cross. 33They came to a place called Golgotha (which means The Place of the Skull). 34There they offered Jesus wine to drink, mixed with gall; but after tasting it, he refused to drink it. 35When they had crucified him, they divided up his clothes by casting lots. 36And sitting down, they kept watch over him there. 37Above his head they placed the written charge against him: THIS IS JESUS, THE KING OF THE JEWS. 38Two robbers were crucified with him, one on his right and one on his left. 39Those who passed by hurled insults at him, shaking their heads 40and saying, "You who are going to destroy the temple and build it in three days, save yourself! Come down from the cross, if you are the Son of God!"

41In the same way the chief priests, the teachers of the law and the elders mocked him. 42"He saved others," they said, "but he can't save himself! He's the King of Israel! Let him come down now from the cross, and we will believe in him. 43He trusts in God. Let God rescue him now if he wants him, for he said, 'I am the Son of God.'" 44In the same way the robbers who were crucified with him also heaped insults on him.

45From the sixth hour until the ninth hour darkness came over all the land. 46About the ninth hour Jesus cried out in a loud voice, "Eloi, Eloi, lama sabachthani?" – which means, "My God, my God, why have you forsaken me?" 47When some of those standing there heard this, they said, "He's calling Elijah." 48Immediately one of them ran and got a sponge. He filled it with wine vinegar, put it on a stick, and offered it to Jesus to drink. 49The rest said, "Now leave him alone. Let's see if Elijah comes to save him." 50And when Jesus had cried out again in a loud voice, he gave up his spirit. 51At that moment the curtain of the temple was torn in two from top to bottom. The earth shook and the rocks split.

Matthew 27:27–51

The symbol of the Christian Faith is not a cradle, to remind us of the much-loved Christmas story, nor a crown, though Jesus claimed to be a king, but a cross. Why? Because the purpose of His coming into the world was to remove the barrier of sin which separated us from God and that could only be done by the sacrifice of Himself.

We have made the cross into a thing of beauty, an ornament and a decoration, but in Jesus' day it was a terrible instrument of torture. And yet we don't sing, as well we might, 'When I survey the monstrous cross', but 'When I survey the wondrous cross'. Why is that? Simply because of what happened there, and in this chapter we see what that was.

We see **what our sins did to Jesus** (46). As in our place He bore the penalty for them, they swept like a thick cloud between Him and His Father, breaking their fellowship, and tearing from His lips that dreadful cry of desolation.

Then we also see **what Jesus did to our sins** (51). The curtain in the temple separated the holiest part of it from the rest, and the splitting of it from top to bottom was a sign that the barrier of sin had been destroyed, that man could be reconciled to God, and that the kingdom of heaven was open to all believers.

Thought: Jesus came to pay a debt He did not owe, because we owed a debt we could not pay.

Prayer

Thank you Lord for:

> 'The love that drew salvation's plan
>
> The grace that brought it down to man,
>
> And the mighty gulf that God did span
>
> At Calvary.' **Amen**

(3) **Prince of Glory**

[3]He was despised and rejected by men,
  a man of sorrows, and familiar with suffering.
  Like one from whom men hide their faces
  he was despised, and we esteemed him not.
[4]Surely he took up our infirmities
  and carried our sorrows,
  yet we considered him stricken by God,
  smitten by him, and afflicted.
[5]But he was pierced for our transgressions,
  he was crushed for our iniquities;
  the punishment that brought us peace was upon him,
  and by his wounds we are healed.
[6]We all, like sheep, have gone astray,
  each of us has turned to his own way;
  and the Lord has laid on him the iniquity of us all.
[7]He was oppressed and afflicted,
  yet he did not open his mouth;
  he was led like a lamb to the slaughter,
  and as a sheep before her shearers is silent,
  so he did not open his mouth.
[8]By oppression and judgment he was taken away.
  And who can speak of his descendants?
  For he was cut off from the land of the living;
  for the transgression of my people he was stricken.
[9]He was assigned a grave with the wicked,
  and with the rich in his death,
  though he had done no violence,
  nor was any deceit in his mouth.
[10]Yet it was the Lord's will to crush him and cause him to suffer,
  and though the Lord makes his life a guilt offering,
  he will see his offspring and prolong his days,
  and the will of the Lord will prosper in his hand.
[11]After the suffering of his soul,
  he will see the light of life and be satisfied;
  by his knowledge my righteous servant will justify many,
  and he will bear their iniquities.
[12]Therefore I will give him a portion among the great,

and he will divide the spoils with the strong,
because he poured out his life unto death,
and was numbered with the transgressors.
For he bore the sin of many,
and made intercession for the transgressors.

Isaiah 53:3–12

This remarkable passage, written hundreds of years before Christ, foreshadows in many details His suffering and death, and is a kind of commentary on what we read yesterday. Notice two phrases in particular.

'Rejected by men' (3). It would not have been surprising if Jesus had been rejected by the Romans or even the Samaritans, but it was His own people who refused Him, and the religious experts who failed to see in Him the 'pearl of great price'.

Their envy and malice and cruelty must have been terribly hard to bear, but we marvel at His courage, His patience and His spirit of forgiveness. It is interesting that the cross has become both the symbol of courage (The Victoria Cross) and of compassion (the Red Cross).

'Stricken by God' (4). But there was a deeper side to the sufferings of Jesus, and a greater pain than even the thorns and the nails; for it was on the cross that Jesus accepted the responsibility, the burden and the guilt of human sin. 'He died that we might be forgiven...'

Look at verse 6. It is said to be the only verse in the Bible beginning and ending with the same word – 'All'. It is like a field with a gate at each end. We all have to go in by the first gate, admitting our need as a sinner; and we can all come out by the second, trusting in Jesus for complete forgiveness.

Thought: In the heavenly courtroom, when I am justly punished for my sins with eternal condemnation, Jesus will get to His feet and present the evidence that my punishment has already been fully executed.

Prayer

I may not know, I cannot tell what pains You had to bear; but I believe it was for me You hung and suffered there. **Amen**

(4) He is Risen

[1]Early on the first day of the week, while it was still dark, Mary Magdalene went to the tomb and saw that the stone had been removed from the entrance. [2]So she came running to Simon Peter and the other disciple, the one Jesus loved, and said, "They have taken the Lord out of the tomb, and we don't know where they have put him!"

[3]So Peter and the other disciple started for the tomb. [4]Both were running, but the other disciple outran Peter and reached the tomb first. [5]He bent over and looked in at the strips of linen lying there but did not go in. [6]Then Simon Peter, who was behind him, arrived and went into the tomb. He saw the strips of linen lying there, [7]as well as the burial cloth that had been around Jesus' head. The cloth was folded up by itself, separate from the linen. [8]Finally the other disciple, who had reached the tomb first, also went inside. He saw and believed.

. . . [19]On the evening of that first day of the week, when the disciples were together, with the doors locked for fear of the Jews, Jesus came and stood among them and said, "Peace be with you!" [20]After he said this, he showed them his hands and side. The disciples were overjoyed when they saw the Lord.

— John 20:1–8, 19-20

During His ministry Jesus brought several people miraculously back to life, but His own experience was quite different. They were revived: He was resurrected. They came back from death, only in due course to die again: He passed through death, to ascend to His Father in heaven.

Many attempts have been made to disprove the resurrection, but none has been able to account for the empty tomb, the missing body, the silence of the authorities (who would have refuted it if they could) and the appearances of Jesus. And what else could have changed the disciples from a demoralised rabble into a victorious army?

The resurrection of Jesus proves two things of great importance. **Jesus is Almighty**. He was 'declared with power to be the Son of God, by His resurrection from the dead' (Romans 1:4). He had conquered sin, Satan and death. We don't yet see everything under His control, but one day we shall, and His ultimate victory is assured by His rising again.

Jesus is alive. At the heart of the Christian faith we don't find a philosophy, a creed or a code of morals. We find a living person, who through His Holy Spirit can be our friend and companion today. '"I am the living one", He says to us, "I was dead, and behold I am alive for ever and ever!"' (Revelation 1:18).

Thought: The stone was rolled away, not to release Jesus, but to reveal the fact that He was risen.

Prayer

Lord Jesus, make Yourself to me a living, bright reality. **Amen**

(5) The Servant King

³Do nothing out of selfish ambition or vain conceit, but in humility consider others better than yourselves. ⁴Each of you should look not only to your own interests, but also to the interests of others.

⁵Your attitude should be the same as that of Christ Jesus:

⁶Who, being in very nature God, did not consider equality with God something to be grasped,

⁷but made himself nothing, taking the very nature of a servant, being made in human likeness.

⁸And being found in appearance as a man, he humbled himself and became obedient to death – even death on a cross! ⁹Therefore God exalted him to the highest place and gave him the name that is above every name,

¹⁰that at the name of Jesus every knee should bow, in heaven and on earth and under the earth,

¹¹and every tongue confess that Jesus Christ is Lord, to the glory of God the Father.

Philippians 2:3-11

This passage starts very simply, reminding us of the danger of self-importance and self-interest, and urging us to be humble; and then suddenly we find ourselves in the middle of a tremendous description of the Incarnation, and how Jesus humbled Himself, and for our sakes became a man, a servant and a criminal.

Think how Jesus might have come – as the Son of God, which He was, surrounded by angels and chariots of fire. Instead He came in poverty, as a refugee, 'a little baby thing who made the women cry.'

Think how Jesus might have lived – as the King, which He was, waited on in a great palace, surrounded by courtiers and retainers. Instead He chose the life of a simple working man, unimportant, and living, not to be served, but to serve others.

Think how Jesus might have died – as the Hero He undoubtedly was, at the head of an army of liberation. Instead He allowed Himself to be betrayed into the hands of wicked men, and to be executed in agony and shame as a common criminal upon a cross.

Why did He come and live and die in this way? Because He put our interests before His own, and our interests meant that He must sacrifice His life to pay the penalty of our sins. He was indeed the great Liberator, but in a way that met our deepest need, and set us free from the prison of sin.

Notice how God exalted Him. He is to be worshipped in two ways – on our knees and with our tongues (10,11) – in obedience and with praise.

Thought: This is our God, the Servant King
He calls us now to follow Him,
To bring our lives as a daily offering
Of worship to the Servant King.
Graham Kendrick © Thankyou Music 1983

Prayer

'May the mind of Christ my Saviour

Live in me from day to day,

By His love and power controlling

All I do and say.' **Amen**

(6) The Gift of God

[1]As for you, you were dead in your transgressions and sins, [2]in which you used to live when you followed the ways of this world and of the ruler of the kingdom of the air, the spirit who is now at work in those who are disobedient. [3]All of us also lived among them at one time, gratifying the cravings of our sinful nature and following its desires and thoughts. Like the rest, we were by nature objects of wrath.

[4]But because of his great love for us, God, who is rich in mercy, [5]made us alive with Christ even when we were dead in transgressions - it is by grace you have been saved. [6]And God raised us up with Christ and seated us with him in the heavenly realms in Christ Jesus, [7]in order that in the coming ages he might show the incomparable riches of his grace, expressed in his kindness to us in Christ Jesus.

[8]For it is by grace you have been saved, through faith -and this not from yourselves, it is the gift of God - [9]not by works, so that no one can boast. [10]For we are God's workmanship, created in Christ Jesus to do good works, which God prepared in advance for us to do.

Ephesians 2:1-10

There are four five-letter words in this passage which sum up its teaching and indeed the Gospel itself. We might put them in the form of a single sentence: 'You are **saved**, not by **works**, but by **grace**, through **faith** for good **works**'.

Saved. A drowning man doesn't need a teacher or an example (though both will have a part to play later), but a rescuer or saviour. As sinners, that is our need, and it was met by Jesus when He died upon the cross.

Works. I cannot earn forgiveness by my good deeds, because they cannot undo the fact that I have broken God's law; nor in the sight of a God who demands perfection, are they good enough. 'For all have sinned and fall short of the glory of God.' (Romans 3:23).

Grace is love, but a special kind of love, for like mercy (4) it can only flow in one direction, from the good to the undeserving, from the great to the humble. I can be courteous to the Queen, but she can be gracious to me. It is like that with God and us.

Faith. This means more than intellectual consent to certain facts ('I believe that...'); it means personal commitment ('I believe in...'). It is the kind of trust we exercise when we put ourselves into the hands of a doctor or a driving instructor.

Deeds / Good **works** may not, as we have seen, earn our forgiveness, but they can express our gratitude; and it is by a new life devoted to them that we show we have responded to God's grace, and that our faith is genuine.

Thought: verse 3 – 'By nature' I was... ; verse 8 – 'by grace' I am... .

Prayer

Lord, You were once a carpenter. Make me a worthy example of your workmanship. **Amen**

(7) A New Creation

[1]Now there was a man of the Pharisees named Nicodemus, a member of the Jewish ruling council. [2]He came to Jesus at night and said, "Rabbi, we know you are a teacher who has come from God. For no one could perform the miraculous signs you are doing if God were not with him."

[3]In reply Jesus declared, "I tell you the truth, no one can see the kingdom of God unless he is born again."

[4]"How can a man be born when he is old?" Nicodemus asked. "Surely he cannot enter a second time into his mother's womb to be born!"

[5]Jesus answered, "I tell you the truth, no one can enter the kingdom of God unless he is born of water and the Spirit. [6]Flesh gives birth to flesh, but the Spirit gives birth to spirit. [7]You should not be surprised at my saying, 'You must be born again.' [8]The wind blows wherever it pleases. You hear its sound, but you cannot tell where it comes from or where it is going. So it is with everyone born of the Spirit."

[9]"How can this be?" Nicodemus asked.

[10]"You are Israel's teacher," said Jesus, "and do you not understand these things? [11]I tell you the truth, we speak of what we know, and we testify to what we have seen, but still you people do not accept our testimony. [12]I have spoken to you of earthly things and you do not believe; how then will you believe if I speak of heavenly things? [13]No one has ever gone into heaven except the one who came from heaven – the Son of Man. [14]Just as Moses lifted up the snake in the desert, so the Son of Man must be lifted up, [15]that everyone who believes in him may have eternal life.

[16]"For God so loved the world that he gave his one and only Son, that whoever believes in him shall not perish but have eternal life."

John 3:1–16

In this midnight conversation, Jesus explained that becoming a Christian involves a change so deep and radical that it can only be described as a 'new birth'. Jesus talked to Nicodemus about physical birth, and then led him on to think about the new spiritual birth which has to happen before anyone can enter the kingdom of God. Just as we cannot appreciate the natural world until we are born into it, so it is only when we are born into God's kingdom that the spiritual world comes alive, and the Bible, prayer, the old familiar hymns and Christian friends begin to mean anything to us.

Verses 14–15 refer to an incident in Numbers 21:6–9 when God punished the rebellious Israelites with a plague of poisonous snakes. Moses was told to set a brass serpent up on a pole, and all who looked at it in faith were healed. Jesus used this to illustrate the way in which forgiveness and life (through the new birth) are available to all who turn and look to Him in faith.

Study verse 16 carefully. It has been called 'the gospel in a nutshell'. Can you find words which describe our great need, God's gracious remedy and what we must do to have eternal life? Remember, eternal life is not just endless existence, but life on a different plane, with a new dimension, which can begin here and now.

Thought: When reading aloud, a child once said 'internal' instead of 'eternal' life. But Jesus actually offers us both.

Prayer

Thank you, Lord, for the newness of life you bring to those who come to know you – new joy, new hope, new strength and peace. **Amen**

(8) Take Up the Cross

[25]Large crowds were travelling with Jesus, and turning to them he said: [26]"If anyone comes to me and does not hate his father and mother, his wife and children, his brothers and sisters – yes, even his own life – he cannot be my disciple. [27]And anyone who does not carry his cross and follow me cannot be my disciple.

[28]"Suppose one of you wants to build a tower. Will he not first sit down and estimate the cost to see if he has enough money to complete it? [29]For if he lays the foundation and is not able to finish it, everyone who sees it will ridicule him, [30]saying, 'This fellow began to build and was not able to finish.'

[31]"Or suppose a king is about to go to war against another king. Will he not first sit down and consider whether he is able with ten thousand men to oppose the one coming against him with twenty thousand? [32]If he is not able, he will send a delegation while the other is still a long way off and will ask for terms of peace. [33]In the same way, any of you who does not give up everything he has cannot be my disciple."

Luke 14:25-33

It has been said that the entrance fee to the kingdom of God is nothing at all, but the daily subscription is all we've got. That is the meaning behind the strong language about hating mothers and fathers and giving up everything in this passage and that is what is meant by 'taking up the cross' – not, as some suppose, being patient when you have toothache, or putting up with a tiresome person at work or in the family. But to take up your cross is to identify yourself wholeheartedly with Jesus Christ and His cause.

The Christian life is like a **building**, Jesus Himself being the foundation stone; and each day we should be adding to it good, solid materials. It is a slow process, and we may wonder at times if we are really growing in our Christian life. But Rome wasn't built in a day, and very often others will see the progress we cannot see, and realize that we are building a Christian character of real worth and value.

The Christian life is also a **battle**, and we are pledged to 'fight manfully against sin, the world and the devil'. The Gulf War of 1991 was described as 'The hundred hours war'. But in 1337 there began the 'Hundred Years War', and that is more like the Christian battle – a life-long struggle: not a sprint, but a marathon.

Both these enterprises are costly, but we are not left alone. Jesus Christ is with us in one case as the Construction expert, and in the other as the Commander; and He will give us the courage and determination we need.

Thought: The Christian life is not a picnic, but a pilgrimage.

Prayer

Teach me, Good Lord, to give and not to count the cost, to fight and not to heed the wounds, to toil and not to seek for rest, to labour and not to ask for any reward, save that of knowing that I do Your will. **Amen**

(9) The Cost of Living

³..."A farmer went out to sow his seed. ⁴As he was scattering the seed, some fell along the path, and the birds came and ate it up. ⁵Some fell on rocky places, where it did not have much soil. It sprang up quickly, because the soil was shallow. ⁶But when the sun came up, the plants were scorched, and they withered because they had no root. ⁷Other seed fell among thorns, which grew up and choked the plants. ⁸Still other seed fell on good soil, where it produced a crop – a hundred, sixty or thirty times what was sown. ⁹He who has ears, let him hear."

...¹⁸"Listen then to what the parable of the sower means: ¹⁹When anyone hears the message about the kingdom and does not understand it, the evil one comes and snatches away what was sown in his heart. This is the seed sown along the path. ²⁰The one who received the seed that fell on rocky places is the man who hears the word and at once receives it with joy. ²¹But since he has no root, he lasts only a short time. When trouble or persecution comes because of the word, he quickly falls away. ²²The one who received the seed that fell among the thorns is the man who hears the word, but the worries of this life and the deceitfulness of wealth choke it, making it unfruitful. ²³But the one who received the seed that fell on good soil is the man who hears the word and understands it. He produces a crop, yielding a hundred, sixty or thirty times what was sown."

Matthew 13:3-9, 18-23

This famous parable illustrates the different responses that people make to the same Gospel message. The sower does his work thoroughly enough, the seed is good, but the trouble lies with the soil. There are four different kinds.

The lighthearted. These people hear a talk, perhaps, which tells how greatly God loves them and explains the claims of Christ. But immediately afterwards, before the message has had a chance to sink in, other things come crowding in and snatch it away. A friend calls, a TV programme 'must' be watched, there is an essay to finish, and by next morning it has 'gone with the wind'.

The fainthearted. These people make a good start, but are not prepared for the opposition – verbal if not physical – which Christians are likely to meet, and because they want to be popular and well-liked, they hide their commitment, and then go back on it all together. They haven't counted the cost.

The halfhearted. Once again there is a good start, but before long the cares and pleasures of the world grow up, fill up all the soil, and smother the message sown in their hearts.

The wholehearted. Here we have a picture of a fruitful, victorious Christian, who gives the message two things which the others deny it – root and room. This person studies the Bible, digging deeply into its soil, and while living a full life doesn't allow hostility to be a disturbance or pleasure to be a distraction.

Thought: 'The trouble with Christianity is not that it has been tried and found wanting, but that it has been found hard and not tried'

G.K. Chesterton

Prayer

Lord, help me to put down deep roots into the soil of your word, and to allow no room for those things which might spoil my fruitfulness. **Amen**

(10) **A Royal Invitation**

¹Jesus entered Jericho and was passing through. ²A man was there by the name of Zacchaeus; he was a chief tax collector and was wealthy. ³He wanted to see who Jesus was, but being a short man he could not, because of the crowd. ⁴So he ran ahead and climbed a sycamore-fig tree to see him, since Jesus was coming that way.

⁵When Jesus reached the spot, he looked up and said to him, "Zacchaeus, come down immediately. I must stay at your house today." ⁶So he came down at once and welcomed him gladly.

⁷All the people saw this and began to mutter, "He has gone to be the guest of a 'sinner.'"

⁸But Zacchaeus stood up and said to the Lord, "Look, Lord! Here and now I give half of my possessions to the poor, and if I have cheated anybody out of anything, I will pay back four times the amount."

⁹Jesus said to him, "Today salvation has come to this house, because this man, too, is a son of Abraham. ¹⁰For the Son of Man came to seek and to save what was lost."

Luke 19:1–10

In the story of Zacchaeus we may perhaps trace the steps by which we became followers of Jesus Christ, and see in his experience a reflection of our own. There were four stages.

A great desire (3). Was it just curiosity that made Zacchaeus so keen to see Jesus? Or was he ashamed of his dishonest life as a tax-collector, and felt that Jesus could help him towards something much better? Or did another tax-collector (Matthew) advise him not to lose the chance of seeing Jesus if He came to Jericho?

A great difficulty (4). Zacchaeus' difficulty was of a practical nature. He simply wasn't tall enough to see Jesus over the crowd in front. He solved his problem in an imaginative way. But Satan always throws obstacles in the way of those trying to escape from his kingdom in order to follow Christ. It could be some simple habit we don't want to abandon, or an unhelpful friendship we would have to break.

A great decision (6). Although there was a decision for Zacchaeus to take, notice that the invitation and the initiative came from Jesus. It is always like that. He calls and we follow. He knocks and we open. Some people can recall the exact moment when they made that response; others can't. But that doesn't matter; the important thing to know is that we have crossed the frontier into His kingdom.

A great difference (8). Zacchaeus knew at once that Christ and sin could not dwell together, and so then and there, at considerable cost to himself, he turned his back on the old way of life, to follow Christ. This is what the Bible calls 'repentance' – a change of attitude towards sin.

Thought: Zacchaeus climbed a sycamore tree to see Jesus (4), but Jesus came all the way from heaven to earth to find Zacchaeus (10).

Prayer

Lord, help me to see where my life should change, now you are my Lord and Master. **Amen**

(11) Springs of Joy

1 Blessed is he
    whose transgressions are forgiven,
    whose sins are covered.
2 Blessed is the man
    whose sin the Lord does not count against him
    and in whose spirit is no deceit.
3 When I kept silent,
    my bones wasted away
    through my groaning all day long.
4 For day and night
    your hand was heavy upon me;
    my strength was sapped
    as in the heat of summer.
5 Then I acknowledged my sin to you
    and did not cover up my iniquity.
    I said, "I will confess
    my transgressions to the Lord" –
    and you forgave
    the guilt of my sin.
6 Therefore let everyone who is godly pray to you
    while you may be found;
    surely when the mighty waters rise,
    they will not reach him.
7 You are my hiding place;
    you will protect me from trouble
    and surround me with songs of deliverance.
8 I will instruct you and teach you in the way you should go;
    I will counsel you and watch over you.
9 Do not be like the horse or the mule,
    which have no understanding
    but must be controlled by bit and bridle
    or they will not come to you.
10 Many are the woes of the wicked,
    but the Lord's unfailing love
    surrounds the man who trusts in him.

¹¹ Rejoice in the Lord and be glad, you righteous;
sing, all you who are upright in heart!

Psalm 32

There is nothing people want more in life than happiness, but so often they look for it in the wrong places, in pleasure, money and even drugs, and come back disappointed. David gives us one great secret of happiness – the forgiveness of sins (1,2); for however much other things may contribute to our happiness, true joy springs from a right relationship with God.

The sin, to which David referred, was the terrible lapse you can read about in 2 Samuel 11, when he committed adultery with Bathsheba and then sent her husband into the thick of the battle to be killed. Like a septic wound it was poisoning his whole life. Finally he did the only thing possible. He could not hide it, or excuse it, so he confessed it (5) to God. Then it was forgiven and covered (1), for God put it away out of sight, out of reach and out of mind (Micah 7:19; Psalm 103:12; Isaiah 43:25).

*Notice three words used to describe wrong-doing. To '**sin**' is to fall short – the old Anglo Saxon word 'synner' was used of someone who missed the mark at archery; '**iniquity**' means to turn aside, out of the straight path; and to '**transgress**' is to trespass, break bounds or go too far.*

*Notice what the Lord meant to David – **Somewhere to hide** (7), a shelter from the storms of temptation and opposition; and **Someone to guide** (8), for like us, David found it very easy to lose his way. Verse 9 tells us of those whom the Lord finds it hard to guide. What sort of people are amenable to His leading? 'He guides the humble in what is right and teaches them His way' (Psalm 25:9).*

Thought: The opposite of joy is not sorrow, but sin.

Prayer

'Lord, be my guardian and my guide

And hear me when I call;

Let not my slippery footsteps slide,

And hold me lest I fall.' **Amen**

23

(12) The Way to Win

¹Then Jesus was led by the Spirit into the desert to be tempted by the devil. ²After fasting forty days and forty nights, he was hungry. ³The tempter came to him and said, "If you are the Son of God, tell these stones to become bread."

⁴Jesus answered, "It is written: 'Man does not live on bread alone, but on every word that comes from the mouth of God.'"

⁵Then the devil took him to the holy city and had him stand on the highest point of the temple. ⁶"If you are the Son of God," he said, "throw yourself down. For it is written:

"'He will command his angels concerning you,

and they will lift you up in their hands,
so that you will not strike your foot against a stone.'"
⁷Jesus answered him, "It is also written: 'Do not put the Lord your God to the test.'"

⁸Again, the devil took him to a very high mountain and showed him all the kingdoms of the world and their splendour. ⁹"All this I will give you," he said, "if you will bow down and worship me."

¹⁰Jesus said to him, "Away from me, Satan! For it is written: 'Worship the Lord your God, and serve him only.'"

¹¹Then the devil left him, and angels came and attended him.

Matthew 4:1-11

'**What makes him tick?**' we sometimes ask of a person. If we apply that question to Jesus, we find that the mainspring of his life was to do the will of God all the time and at any cost; and the temptations in the wilderness were Satan's attempt to divert him from this course. 'Be a great economist', he said, 'and solve the world's social problems at a stroke' (3). 'Be a great entertainer, and you will have the world at your feet; (5,6,). 'Be a great emperor, and put an end to war and oppression' (8,9). What attractive options! But Jesus refused to be distracted, and each temptation was met with a reference to Scripture, reminding us how important a knowledge of the Bible is if we are to overcome temptation. 'I have hidden your word in my heart that I might not sin against you' (Psalm 119:11).

What other lessons are there for us? Satan may not be able to tempt us to commit some gross sin (though he is likely to try), but he is sure to try to distract us from the path of wholehearted allegiance to Christ. Very often success is more damaging to our Christian lives than sin. Sin should drive us back to Christ for forgiveness, but success can make us think we can manage quite well without Him.

We are warned here against three kinds of success: Prosperity (3), Popularity (5,6) and Power (8,9). We are not told to avoid these things if they come our way, and in its right place each may be enjoyed and used. But to seek them for their own sake, to allow them to become the things that 'make us tick', can be Satan's way of turning us into second-class Christians.

Thought: Temptations begin with a question – 'If... ?' Victories begin with a quotation – 'It is written...'.

Prayer

'Still let me ever watch and pray, and feel that I am frail,
That if the tempter cross my way, yet he may not prevail'. **Amen**

(13) We Shall Overcome

²Consider it pure joy, my brothers, whenever you face trials of many kinds, ³because you know that the testing of your faith develops perseverance. ⁴Perseverance must finish its work so that you may be mature and complete, not lacking anything. ⁵If any of you lacks wisdom, he should ask God, who gives generously to all without finding fault, and it will be given to him. ⁶But when he asks, he must believe and not doubt, because he who doubts is like a wave of the sea, blown and tossed by the wind. ⁷That man should not think he will receive anything from the Lord; ⁸he is a double-minded man, unstable in all he does....

¹²Blessed is the man who perseveres under trial, because when he has stood the test, he will receive the crown of life that God has promised to those who love him.

¹³When tempted, no one should say, "God is tempting me." For God cannot be tempted by evil, nor does he tempt anyone; ¹⁴but each one is tempted when, by his own evil desire, he is dragged away and enticed. ¹⁵Then, after desire has conceived, it gives birth to sin; and sin, when it is full-grown, gives birth to death....

²²Do not merely listen to the word, and so deceive yourselves. Do what it says. ²³Anyone who listens to the word but does not do what it says is like a man who looks at his face in a mirror ²⁴and, after looking at himself, goes away and immediately forgets what he looks like. ²⁵But the man who looks intently into the perfect law that gives freedom, and continues to do this, not forgetting what he has heard, but doing it – he will be blessed in what he does.

James 1:2-9, 12-15, 22-25

This chapter has some very practical things to say about trials and temptations.

We must expect them *(13,14) for they are part of our common heritage. 'No temptation has seized you except what is common to man. And God is faithful; he will not let you be tempted beyond what you can bear. But when you are tempted, he will also provide a way out so that you can stand up under it.' (1 Corinthians 10:13). The Christian is nowhere promised immunity, rather the reverse.*

We must enjoy them *(2). Isn't that pushing it a bit far? Well, it is the attitude of a committed athlete when he or she faces a particularly gruelling physical test with enthusiasm. It is the point Paul seemed to reach: 'Therefore I will boast all the more gladly about my weaknesses, so that Christ's power may rest on me. That is why, for Christ's sake, I delight in weaknesses, in insults, in hardships, in persecutions, in difficulties. For when I am weak, then I am strong.' (2 Corinthians 12:9-10). It gives us a chance to prove the power of Christ in our lives.*

We must endure them *(12). We can never be sure when or where the attacks will come, but with the power of Christ we will be able to overcome.*

James mentions two other things – two 'means of grace' or channels through which God's strength will reach us: Prayer (5–7) and Bible reading (21–25). Make good use of them.

Thought: 'We must always be ready to meet at our average moment anything that any possible enemy may hurl against us at his selected moment.'

Sir Winston Churchill

Prayer

I thank you, O Lord, that every trial and temptation provides an opportunity to put Your strength to the test. **Amen**

(14) **The Armour of Light** ────────────────

[10]Finally, be strong in the Lord and in his mighty power. [11]Put on the full armour of God so that you can take your stand against the devil's schemes. [12]For our struggle is not against flesh and blood, but against the rulers, against the authorities, against the powers of this dark world and against the spiritual forces of evil in the heavenly realms.

[13]Therefore put on the full armour of God, so that when the day of evil comes, you may be able to stand your ground, and after you have done everything, to stand. [14]Stand firm then, with the belt of truth buckled around your waist, with the breastplate of righteousness in place, [15]and with your feet fitted with the readiness that comes from the gospel of peace. [16]In addition to all this, take up the shield of faith, with which you can extinguish all the flaming arrows of the evil one. [17]Take the helmet of salvation and the sword of the Spirit, which is the word of God. [18]And pray in the Spirit on all occasions with all kinds of prayers and requests. With this in mind, be alert and always keep on praying for all the saints.

[19]Pray also for me, that whenever I open my mouth, words may be given me so that I will fearlessly make known the mystery of the gospel, [20]for which I am an ambassador in chains. Pray that I may declare it fearlessly, as I should.

──────────────────────────────── *Ephesians 6:10-20*

Paul liked to compare the Christian to a soldier, and in this chapter he gives us two different pictures of him.

In action. Notice (a) **The enemy** (12). We are not fighting a human war, but a spiritual one, against the powers of darkness, master-minded by Satan, which control the minds of men and women throughout the world. The battle has already been won, through the death and resurrection of Jesus, but a wild beast is never more dangerous than when it is mortally wounded; and Satan is like that.

(b) **The equipment** (13–17). From time to time it is wise to make sure that each piece of armour is in place, because if something is missing, Satan could get an advantage over us. Notice the one offensive weapon – 'the sword of the Spirit'. For us that is the Bible, and to know it well and to apply it to different situations is the secret of victory.

On guard. The Christian is never 'off duty', and almost the last command that Jesus gave His disciples was to 'watch and pray' lest they enter into temptation (Matthew 26:41); and sometimes when we are off our guard, temptation can creep up on us. To **'pray'** is to keep an eye on our friend knowing that His power is at our disposal; to **'watch'** is to keep an eye on our enemy, and his possible points of attack.

Thought: The price of freedom is eternal vigilance.

Prayer

Lord, give me strength manfully to fight under Your banner against sin, the world and the devil, and to continue as Your faithful soldier until the end of my life. **Amen**

(15) Walking in the Light

[5]This is the message we have heard from him and declare to you: God is light; in him there is no darkness at all. [6]If we claim to have fellowship with him yet walk in the darkness, we lie and do not live by the truth. [7]But if we walk in the light, as he is in the light, we have fellowship with one another, and the blood of Jesus, his Son, purifies us from all sin.

[8]If we claim to be without sin, we deceive ourselves and the truth is not in us. [9]If we confess our sins, he is faithful and just and will forgive us our sins and purify us from all unrighteousness. [10]If we claim we have not sinned, we make him out to be a liar and his word has no place in our lives.

[2:1]My dear children, I write this to you so that you will not sin. But if anybody does sin, we have one who speaks to the Father in our defence – Jesus Christ, the Righteous One. [2]He is the atoning sacrifice for our sins, and not only for ours but also for the sins of the whole world.

1 John 1:5–2:2

In this letter John deals helpfully with some of the questions, to which those beginning the Christian life want an answer. What should be my attitude towards sin? Will I still fall into temptation? What happens if I do? Notice three things that are mentioned here.

The practice of sin (6). One of the signs that we really belong to Christ is that we shall not want to 'walk in darkness', that is, continue to practice those things which we know to be wrong. A little later, in verse 9 of chapter 3, John says that the Christian 'cannot sin'. He doesn't mean that he never will, but there will be certain things about which he says, 'I can't do that', because it would be displeasing to Christ.

The possibility of sin (8). But within our hearts there still remains the old, sinful nature, and we shall deceive ourselves and deny what God has said (10) if forgetting this we imagine that failure is no longer possible. However far we advance in the Christian life, it will never be impossible for us to sin. We cannot eradicate the old nature, but we have to learn to counteract it.

The pardon of sin (9). If we do fall, God does not cast us out ("All that the father gives me will come to me, and whoever comes to me I will never drive away." John 6:37), and we don't have to start the Christian life all over again. Our relationship with God will remain intact, but our friendship will be damaged and spoiled. But as soon as we confess our sins, He is ready to forgive, and to encourage us on our way again ('. . . though he stumble, he will not fall, for the Lord upholds him with his hand.' Psalm 37:24).

Thought: If we do fall, it is important to remember to fall the right way – on to our knees.

Prayer

'O wonder of all wonders, that through your death for me
My open sins, my secret sins, can all forgiven be.' **Amen**

(16) **The School of Prayer**

¹One day Jesus was praying in a certain place. When he finished, one of his disciples said to him, "Lord, teach us to pray, just as John taught his disciples."

²He said to them, "When you pray, say:
'Father,
hallowed be your name,
your kingdom come.

³Give us each day our daily bread.

⁴Forgive us our sins,
for we also forgive everyone who sins against us.
And lead us not into temptation.'

⁵Then he said to them, "Suppose one of you has a friend, and he goes to him at midnight and says, 'Friend, lend me three loaves of bread, ⁶because a friend of mine on a journey has come to me, and I have nothing to set before him.'

⁷"Then the one inside answers, 'Don't bother me. The door is already locked, and my children are with me in bed. I can't get up and give you anything.' ⁸I tell you, though he will not get up and give him the bread because he is his friend, yet because of the man's boldness he will get up and give him as much as he needs.

⁹"So I say to you: Ask and it will be given to you; seek and you will find; knock and the door will be opened to you. ¹⁰For everyone who asks receives; he who seeks finds; and to him who knocks, the door will be opened.

¹¹"Which of you fathers, if your son asks for a fish, will give him a snake instead? ¹²Or if he asks for an egg, will give him a scorpion? ¹³If you then, though you are evil, know how to give good gifts to your children, how much more will your Father in heaven give the Holy Spirit to those who ask him!"

— Luke 11:1-13

Perhaps the disciples had begun to see that there was a connection between the power Jesus displayed and the lonely times of prayer He spent on the hills, and one day they came to Him and asked, 'Lord teach us to pray'. Like all good lessons, the one that followed contained an explanation, an illustration and an application.

Explanation *(2–4). Prayer is talking to God, and in 'The Lord's Prayer', as we call it, we see three essential attitudes we must adopt: Reverence ('hallowed...'), Penitence ('forgive...') and Dependence ('give...'). It is in this way that we must always approach God.*

Illustration *(5–8, 11–13). God wants us to think of Him as a Friend and a Father, as these two illustrations suggest. The argument is one known in the legal world as 'a fortiori'. If a lazy, unwilling friend can be persuaded to help, how much more will God do so, who knows our needs before we ask, and is able to give more than we desire or deserve? And if an ordinary, sinful father knows what is good for his children, how much more may we rely upon God to meet our needs?*

Application *(9–10). The words 'Ask – Seek – Knock' suggest simplicity, intensity and persistence. Perhaps some prayers are not granted because God doesn't see more than a passing desire in our hearts for the thing we ask for, and, like a wise father, He waits to see if we are in earnest.*

Thought: Prayer doesn't change God's mind. But it opens His hand.

Prayer

Lord, please enrol me in your school, and teach me to pray. **Amen**

(17) Under New Management

¹Therefore, I urge you, brothers, in view of God's mercy, to offer your bodies as living sacrifices, holy and pleasing to God – this is your spiritual act of worship. ²Do not conform any longer to the pattern of this world, but be transformed by the renewing of your mind. Then you will be able to test and approve what God's will is – his good, pleasing and perfect will....

⁹Love must be sincere. Hate what is evil; cling to what is good. ¹⁰Be devoted to one another in brotherly love. Honour one another above yourselves. ¹¹Never be lacking in zeal, but keep your spiritual fervour, serving the Lord. ¹²Be joyful in hope, patient in affliction, faithful in prayer. ¹³Share with God's people who are in need. Practice hospitality.

¹⁴Bless those who persecute you; bless and do not curse. ¹⁵Rejoice with those who rejoice; mourn with those who mourn. ¹⁶Live in harmony with one another. Do not be proud, but be willing to associate with people of low position. Do not be conceited.

¹⁷Do not repay anyone evil for evil. Be careful to do what is right in the eyes of everybody. ¹⁸If it is possible, as far as it depends on you, live at peace with everyone. ¹⁹Do not take revenge, my friends, but leave room for God's wrath, for it is written: "It is mine to avenge; I will repay," says the Lord.

²⁰On the contrary:
"If your enemy is hungry, feed him;
if he is thirsty, give him something to drink.
In doing this, you will heap burning coals on his head."

²¹Do not be overcome by evil, but overcome evil with good.

Romans 12:1-2, 9–21

The Christian is someone who has been transferred ('from the dominion of darkness... into the kingdom of the Son' Colossians 1:13) that he may be transformed. Imagine a Frenchman who becomes a naturalised Englishman. He becomes an Englishman at once, but it will take him many years to become 'English'. Becoming a Christian is a crisis; becoming Christ-like is a process. We are transformed slowly and sometimes painfully over a life-time. This chapter tells us what it will mean.

Our bodies (1) must be yielded to God as instruments for His service. 'Do not offer the parts of your body to sin, as instruments of wickedness, but rather offer yourselves to God, as those who have been brought from death to life; and offer the parts of your body to him as instruments of righteousness (Romans 3:13). For God wants our energy, our talents, our enthusiasm to fulfil His purposes in the world. Such a 'living sacrifice' on our part should seem to be no more than our 'reasonable service' in the light of all He has done for us.

Our minds (2). The 'renewal' or 'transforming' of our minds will show itself in new attitudes. Notice four: **Efficiency** in our work (11), because we are doing it to please Him; **Sympathy** towards others (15) in their joys and sorrows; **Humility**, which shows itself when we refuse to stand on our dignity (16) or to resent being overtaken by others; and **Honesty** in all our dealings with other people (17).

Thought: the great paradox of the Christian life is this: That we must seek to become what we already are.

Prayer

Take me as I am, Lord, and make me all your own;
Make my heart your palace, and your royal throne. **Amen**

(18) **Newness of Life**

[1]Since, then, you have been raised with Christ, set your hearts on things above, where Christ is seated at the right hand of God. [2]Set your minds on things above, not on earthly things. [3]For you died, and your life is now hidden with Christ in God. [4]When Christ, who is your life, appears, then you also will appear with him in glory....

[12]Therefore, as God's chosen people, holy and dearly loved, clothe yourselves with compassion, kindness, humility, gentleness and patience. [13]Bear with each other and forgive whatever grievances you may have against one another. Forgive as the Lord forgave you. [14]And over all these virtues put on love, which binds them all together in perfect unity.

[15]Let the peace of Christ rule in your hearts, since as members of one body you were called to peace. And be thankful. [16]Let the word of Christ dwell in you richly as you teach and admonish one another with all wisdom, and as you sing psalms, hymns and spiritual songs with gratitude in your hearts to God. [17]And whatever you do, whether in word or deed, do it all in the name of the Lord Jesus, giving thanks to God the Father through him.

Colossians 3:1–4, 12–17

The Christian is really a kind of 'colonist' on this earth. That is to say, our proper home is in heaven with Christ (1-4), and that is where our affections should be centred, and where our fortune and our treasure are stored, awaiting our eventual arrival.

But just as a person will often reveal his home country by his dress or speech, so we as Christians betray ourselves and our real spiritual nationality. **Our dress.** *We thought recently about the Christian's armour, but today we are concerned with our 'civilian clothes' – the way we present ourselves, not to the enemy, but to our friends and acquaintances. The 'clothing list' (12-14) deserves careful study, and it includes all those things which supremely adorned the life of Christ.*

Our speech. *Our speech also betrays us, and you can often tell what country a person comes from, and even what part of a country by his accent. As Christians, we will be known by the wisdom (16), with which we speak, our willingness to forgive (13), our cheerfulness (16) and our gratitude (17).*

There ought to be something about the Christian's dress and 'accent' that will make other people want to know more about the kingdom, to which we belong, and the nature of our homeland.

Thought: If you were on trial for being a Christian, would there be enough evidence to convict you?

Prayer

Lord, may there be something about me that will remind other people about You. **Amen**

(19) On His Majesty's Service

[14]For Christ's love compels us, because we are convinced that one died for all, and therefore all died. [15]And he died for all, that those who live should no longer live for themselves but for him who died for them and was raised again.

[16]So from now on we regard no one from a worldly point of view. Though we once regarded Christ in this way, we do so no longer. [17]Therefore, if anyone is in Christ, he is a new creation; the old has gone, the new has come!

[18]All this is from God, who reconciled us to himself through Christ and gave us the ministry of reconciliation: [19]that God was reconciling the world to himself in Christ, not counting men's sins against them. And he has committed to us the message of reconciliation.

[20]We are therefore Christ's ambassadors, as though God were making his appeal through us. We implore you on Christ's behalf: Be reconciled to God. [21]God made him who had no sin to be sin for us, so that in him we might become the righteousness of God.

— 2 Corinthians 5:14–21

'That those who live should no longer live for themselves but for him who died for them...' (15). Those words sum up this passage, the rest of which develops the theme of service for Christ.

Our motive (14). People are motivated to serve for many different reasons – duty, fear, reward and so on; but the highest motive must surely be love. The word translated 'compel' here reminds us that the love of Christ has a dynamic as well as a magnetic power. It draws us to Jesus ("I, when I am lifted up from the earth, will draw all men to myself." John12:32). But then it drives us out in His service as well.

Our message (19). We have marvellous news to pass on – that peace has been made between man and God. The 'iron curtain' of sin which hung between us has been removed through the death of Christ upon the cross. The fine has been cancelled, the debt paid, the door opened, and we are reconciled to God.

Our method (20). The form of service we are offered is very privileged, for we are called to be 'ambassadors for Christ'. He took our place upon the cross, and He now asks us to take His place in the world. An ambassador is a representative, and others will judge our king by the way we live; and he is also a foreigner, and we must not be surprised to find that the world has different standards, different values and a different language from us. It will not be easy to be fully involved with the world and yet not be assimilated by it Jesus prayed for His disciples, "My prayer is not that you take them out of the world but that you protect them from the evil one." John 17:15).

Thought: The ambassador's motto: 'Not isolated, but insulated.'

Prayer

Lord Jesus, make me a channel of Your peace. **Amen**

(20) Neighbours!

²⁵On one occasion an expert in the law stood up to test Jesus. "Teacher," he asked, "what must I do to inherit eternal life?"

²⁶"What is written in the Law?" he replied. "How do you read it?"

²⁷He answered: "'Love the Lord your God with all your heart and with all your soul and with all your strength and with all your mind'; and, 'Love your neighbour as yourself.'"

²⁸"You have answered correctly," Jesus replied. "Do this and you will live."

²⁹But he wanted to justify himself, so he asked Jesus, "And who is my neighbour?"

³⁰In reply Jesus said: "A man was going down from Jerusalem to Jericho, when he fell into the hands of robbers. They stripped him of his clothes, beat him and went away, leaving him half dead. ³¹A priest happened to be going down the same road, and when he saw the man, he passed by on the other side. ³²So too, a Levite, when he came to the place and saw him, passed by on the other side.

³³"But a Samaritan, as he travelled, came where the man was; and when he saw him, he took pity on him. ³⁴He went to him and bandaged his wounds, pouring on oil and wine. Then he put the man on his own donkey, took him to an inn and took care of him. ³⁵The next day he took out two silver coins and gave them to the innkeeper. 'Look after him,' he said, 'and when I return, I will reimburse you for any extra expense you may have.'"

Luke 10:25-35

Jesus told this story to show the lawyer what is meant by 'neighbourly love', and explained that it is not just something we must exercise towards friends and family, but towards strangers, foreigners and even, as in this case, members of a hostile country. This sort of service is often costly, and it involved the Good Samaritan in three things.

Daring. How was he to know that the victim was not a decoy? Or that bandits were not waiting in the hills to attack the next lonely traveller? He took a risk, and that may have been what deterred the Priest and the Levite. It does take courage sometimes to befriend the unpopular, or to champion the underdog.

Caring. He 'took pity on him'. He didn't just feel sorry as we do when we read of atrocities in the newspaper; he took firm, positive, practical action, and went to the man's help.

Sharing. Having loved with his **heart**, and shown pity, he now loved with his **mind** and made a plan, and then with his **strength**, using his physical energy to get the man safely to an inn, sharing his transport and his money. God has given us all certain gifts which we can either hoard for ourselves, or use for the benefit of others, often at some cost to ourselves.

Thought: 'No man is an island.'

John Donne

Prayer

Lord, give me the courage, the compassion and the capacity to love my neighbour as myself. **Amen**

(21) The King of Love

¹The Lord is my shepherd, I shall not be in want.

²He makes me lie down in green pastures,
      he leads me beside quiet waters,

³ he restores my soul.
      He guides me in paths of righteousness
      for his name's sake.

⁴Even though I walk
      through the valley of the shadow of death,
      I will fear no evil,
      for you are with me;
      your rod and your staff,
      they comfort me.

⁵You prepare a table before me
      in the presence of my enemies.
      You anoint my head with oil;
      my cup overflows.

⁶Surely goodness and love will follow me
      all the days of my life,
      and I will dwell in the house of the Lord
      forever.

Psalm 23

---

¹¹"I am the good shepherd. The good shepherd lays down his life for the sheep. . . ¹⁴I am the good shepherd; I know my sheep and my sheep know me –... ²⁷My sheep listen to my voice; I know them, and they follow me. ²⁸I give them eternal life, and they shall never perish; no one can snatch them out of my hand. ²⁹My Father, who has given them to me, is greater than all; no one can snatch them out of my Father's hand."

John 10:11,14,27-29

This matchless little Psalm, probably the best-known, and the best-loved in the world, has been said to describe 'a day in the life of a sheep'. When we come to know the Shepherd, there is no part of it which we won't be able to relate to our own experience, and which will not help us at some time or other in our journey through the Christian life.

Notice the four different scenes:
Pastures (2) suggest the sense of peace and satisfaction which Christ can provide for His followers.
Paths (3). But the Christian is more than a follower, for there are 'paths of righteousness' which we must find and walk. Often this is not easy, and without Christ as our guide, we could easily go wrong and 'err and stray from His ways like lost sheep'.
Valleys (4). Sometimes our path dips away from the sunshine, and we find ourselves in the valley of disappointment or failure or trouble, and one day 'the shadow of death'. But what a difference it can make if the Shepherd is with us!
The house (6). This is a picture of heaven, and speaks of something permanent and secure, unlike the tents which were so common in those days. It is the place to which every Christian can look forward with steadfast hope.

The verses from John's gospel form an interesting commentary on the Psalm. Notice two things in particular about the Good Shepherd.
His voice (27). We must always be tuned into the voice of Jesus as He speaks to us through the Bible, through conscience or even through Christian friends.
His hand (28). If it is the Shepherd's voice that guides us, it is His hand that guards us in times of danger and temptation.

Thought: When you can't sleep, don't count sheep. Try talking to the Shepherd.

Prayer

Lord Jesus, please be my shepherd all the days of my life, and when I walk through the valley of the shadow of death may I fear no evil, because You are with me – leading me to the glory of heaven. **Amen**

(22) Faith Under Fire

[1]Peter, an apostle of Jesus Christ, To God's elect, strangers in the world, scattered throughout Pontus, Galatia, Cappadocia, Asia and Bithynia, [2]who have been chosen according to the foreknowledge of God the Father, through the sanctifying work of the Spirit, for obedience to Jesus Christ and sprinkling by his blood:

Grace and peace be yours in abundance.

[3]Praise be to the God and Father of our Lord Jesus Christ! In his great mercy he has given us new birth into a living hope through the resurrection of Jesus Christ from the dead, [4]and into an inheritance that can never perish, spoil or fade – kept in heaven for you, [5]who through faith are shielded by God's power until the coming of the salvation that is ready to be revealed in the last time.

[6]In this you greatly rejoice, though now for a little while you may have had to suffer grief in all kinds of trials. [7]These have come so that your faith – of greater worth than gold, which perishes even though refined by fire – may be proved genuine and may result in praise, glory and honour when Jesus Christ is revealed. [8]Though you have not seen him, you love him; and even though you do not see him now, you believe in him and are filled with an inexpressible and glorious joy, [9]for you are receiving the goal of your faith, the salvation of your souls.

1 Peter 1:1–9

When we begin the Christian life, we are 'born again' into God's family, and we inherit our share of the family fortune which is reserved for us in heaven – the salvation of our souls. But is our salvation still future? Surely it is something we can enjoy here and now?

There are three tenses of salvation.

Past. *When we first put our trust in Christ, and invited Him into our hearts, we were saved or delivered from the guilt of sin and its penalty, which Christ bore in our place.*

Present. *As we trust in Him day by day, and obey His commands, we can be delivered continuously from the power of sin. It need and should no longer have dominion over us. 'For sin shall not be your master, because you are not under law, but under grace' (Romans 6:14).*

Future. *Finally one day, when we go to be with Christ, our salvation will be complete, for we shall be delivered from the very presence of sin, and feel its power no more. 'Nothing impure will ever enter it [the city of God], nor will anyone who does what is shameful or deceitful, but only those whose names are written in the Lamb's book of life.' (Revelation 21:27).*

The Christian is like someone who inherits a fortune. There is an outright gift, we will suppose, which pays off all his debts; a steady, assured income for life; and then, on reaching a certain age, the full possession of his property.

Notice three familiar words in this passage – Faith, Hope and Love. Each plays a part in our salvation. Faith looks back in gratitude to what Christ did on the cross, and trusts in that day by day for forgiveness. Hope looks forward to the day when we shall see Jesus face to face. The love of God for us is poured into our hearts by the Holy Spirit, and in response to that wonderful love we love Him back, and begin to be able to love our neighbour as ourselves.

Thought: 'Now faith is being sure of what we hope for and certain of what we do not see.'(Hebrews 11:1).

Prayer

We thank You, O Lord, that You have prepared for them that love You such good things as pass man's understanding. **Amen**

(23) **The Slough of Despond** —————————

[1]As the deer pants for streams of water,
>so my soul pants for you, O God.

[2]My soul thirsts for God, for the living God.
>When can I go and meet with God?

[3]My tears have been my food day and night,
>while men say to me all day long, "Where is your God?"

[4]These things I remember
>as I pour out my soul:
>how I used to go with the multitude,
>leading the procession to the house of God,
>with shouts of joy and thanksgiving
>among the festive throng.

[5]Why are you downcast, O my soul?
>Why so disturbed within me?
>Put your hope in God,
>for I will yet praise him,
>my Saviour and [6] my God.
>My soul is downcast within me;
>therefore I will remember you
>from the land of the Jordan,
>the heights of Hermon – from Mount Mizar.

[7]Deep calls to deep
>in the roar of your waterfalls;
>all your waves and breakers have swept over me.

[8]By day the Lord directs his love,
>at night his song is with me – a prayer to the God of my life.

[9]I say to God my Rock,
>"Why have you forgotten me?
>Why must I go about mourning, oppressed by the enemy?"

[10]My bones suffer mortal agony as my foes taunt me,
>saying to me all day long, "Where is your God?"

[11]Why are you downcast, O my soul?
>Why so disturbed within me?
>Put your hope in God, for I will yet praise him,
>my Saviour and my God.

—————————————————————————————— *Psalm 42*

We don't know the exact circumstances in which this Psalm was written, but it would be a very unusual Christian who has never found that this Psalm matched his or her own mood at times, and who has never experienced a time of spiritual doubt and depression, sometimes called 'the dark night of the soul'.

Notice the two questions which disturb the writer:

Where is your God? (3). There will be times when people will challenge our belief in God, and suggest that we are simply chasing the wind.

Why have you forgotten me? (9). And there will be times when we ourselves wonder whether God has not lost interest and control of the world and of His people.

The psalmist's remedy is threefold:

To remember (4). Go over in your mind all the good things that God has done for you and remind yourself of what He is still doing in other places and among other people.

To praise (8). This will lead you to thank and praise Him. If other forms of prayer are proving difficult, then switch to praise – and the rest will come more easily.

To wait (11). To 'wait on God' is a favourite idea in the Psalms. It means we are dependent (like a child on its mother); obedient (like a good waiter in a restaurant); and it means we are expectant (like someone waiting for a friend to arrive). If you find yourself in Bunyan's 'Slough of Despond', try (in spite of every feeling to the contrary) to cultivate this attitude, even out of a sense of duty, and the joy will return.

Thought: Turn your face to the sunshine, and the shadows will fall behind.

Prayer

When all your mercies, O my God,

My rising soul surveys,

Transported with the view I'm lost

In wonder, love and praise. **Amen**

(24) Renewal

18To whom, then, will you compare God?
What image will you compare him to?...

21Do you not know?
Have you not heard?
Has it not been told you from the beginning?
Have you not understood since the earth was founded?

22He sits enthroned above the circle of the earth,
and its people are like grasshoppers.
He stretches out the heavens like a canopy,
and spreads them out like a tent to live in.

23He brings princes to naught
and reduces the rulers of this world to nothing.

24No sooner are they planted,
no sooner are they sown,
no sooner do they take root in the ground,
than he blows on them and they wither,
and a whirlwind sweeps them away like chaff.

25"To whom will you compare me?
Or who is my equal?" says the Holy One.

26Lift your eyes and look to the heavens:
Who created all these?
He who brings out the starry host one by one,
and calls them each by name.
Because of his great power and mighty strength,
not one of them is missing.

27Why do you say, O Jacob,
and complain, O Israel,
"My way is hidden from the Lord;
my cause is disregarded by my God"?

28Do you not know?
Have you not heard?
The Lord is the everlasting God,
the Creator of the ends of the earth.
He will not grow tired or weary,
and his understanding no one can fathom.

29He gives strength to the weary
and increases the power of the weak.

³⁰Even youths grow tired and weary,
    and young men stumble and fall;
³¹but those who hope in the Lord
    will renew their strength.
    They will soar on wings like eagles;
    they will run and not grow weary,
    they will walk and not be faint.

Isaiah 40:18, 21–31

What is God like? *That is the oldest and deepest question man has asked, and in one sense it is unanswerable, for the Bible tells us that 'God is light', and you can only see light if you pass it through a prism, and break it up into the component colours of the spectrum. Jesus is the prism through whom we see what God is like. In His life, we see God's holiness; in His teaching, God's wisdom; in His miracles, God's power; and in His cross, we see God's love. That is what Jesus meant when He said, 'Anyone who has seen me has seen the Father' (John 14:9). Can you see glimpses of these qualities in today's passage?*

Look at the last two verses. Have you ever fainted? If so, it was probably due to one of three things – Heat, Hunger or Haemorrhage! All too often we faint in the Christian life for these reasons. Perhaps we find the pace too hot, the opposition too strong and the ridicule too much to bear. Or perhaps we don't give ourselves time to feed upon the Bible and to build up our spiritual strength. Or again, we may fall badly into temptation, lose a lot of spiritual blood, and feel it isn't worth going on.

God's answer in each case is to wait on the Lord – to spend time with Him, just as a battery has to wait if it is to be recharged, or a patient who is having a blood-transfusion. Then notice what happens. Our spiritual vitality and youthfulness are restored and renewed.

Thought: The Olympic motto is 'Swifter, Higher, Stronger.' (verse 31).

Prayer

Lord, help me to obey Your command that 'Men ought always to pray, and not to faint'. When I fail, forgive me and renew me. **Amen**

(25) More Than Conquerors

^{28}And we know that in all things God works for the good of those who love him, who have been called according to his purpose. ^{29}For those God foreknew he also predestined to be conformed to the likeness of his Son, that he might be the firstborn among many brothers. ^{30}And those he predestined, he also called; those he called, he also justified; those he justified, he also glorified.

^{31}What then, shall we say in response to this? If God is for us, who can be against us? ^{32}He who did not spare his own Son, but gave him up for us all – how will he not also, along with him, graciously give us all things? ^{33}Who will bring any charge against those whom God has chosen? It is God who justifies. ^{34}Who is he that condemns? Christ Jesus, who died – more than that, who was raised to life – is at the right hand of God and is also interceding for us. ^{35}Who shall separate us from the love of Christ? Shall trouble or hardship or persecution or famine or nakedness or danger or sword? ^{36}As it is written:

> "For your sake we face death all day long;
> we are considered as sheep to be slaughtered."

^{37}No, in all these things we are more than conquerors through him who loved us. ^{38}For I am convinced that neither death nor life, neither angels nor demons, neither the present nor the future, nor any powers, ^{39}neither height nor depth, nor anything else in all creation, will be able to separate us from the love of God that is in Christ Jesus our Lord.

Romans 8:28-39

Three times in these verses there appears the words, 'all things'.

Verse 28. *'And we know that in all things God works for the good of those who love him, who have been called according to his purpose'. Here we have a very encouraging promise, for we are assured that for the Christian there is no such thing as chance. Sorrow as well as joy, sickness as well as health, can be part of God's plan for us. He often uses the black notes as well as the white to produce the best music from our lives. Read of one man to whom this happened in Genesis 50:19–21.*

Verse 32. *'He who did not spare his own Son, but gave him up for us all – how will he not also, along with him, graciously give us all things?' God has already given us His greatest and most precious gift – His Son to be our Saviour and Friend. How much more, therefore, will He give us other lesser things which we shall need in the Christian life? So when you feel the need for courage, wisdom, patience, or whatever it may be, you can confidently ask Him to give it to you.*

Verse 37. *'No, in all these things we are more than conquerors through him who loved us.' The Christian is not above the Master, and we must not expect to escape hardship. In a world which is largely hostile to Christ, we must be prepared to be misunderstood and opposed. It happened to Jesus, and He warned us it would happen to us – "I have told you these things, so that in me you may have peace. In this world you will have trouble. But take heart! I have overcome the world"(John 16:33). But we must not allow such things to dismay us. They are not a sign that God has withdrawn His love. He allows us to be tempted, tested and tried that we may emerge all the stronger and more useful. "12Dear friends, do not be surprised at the painful trial you are suffering, as though something strange were happening to you. 13But rejoice that you participate in the sufferings of Christ, so that you may be overjoyed when His glory is revealed. 14If you are insulted because of the name of Christ, you are blessed, for the Spirit of glory and of God rests on you.'(1 Peter 4:12–14).*

Thought: Christ helps us to face the music, even when we don't like the tune.

Prayer

> Lord God, I praise You and thank You that You can work for my good in all the things that happen to me, whatever they are, and however hard they may seem to be. Your will be done, Lord. **Amen**

(26) Experience Will Decide

[1]I will extol the Lord at all times;
>his praise will always be on my lips.
[2]My soul will boast in the Lord;
>let the afflicted hear and rejoice.
[3]Glorify the Lord with me;
>let us exalt his name together.
[4]I sought the Lord, and he answered me;
>he delivered me from all my fears.
[5]Those who look to him are radiant;
>their faces are never covered with shame.
[6]This poor man called, and the Lord heard him;
>he saved him out of all his troubles.
[7]The angel of the Lord encamps around those who fear him,
>and he delivers them.
[8]Taste and see that the Lord is good;
>blessed is the man who takes refuge in him.
[9]Fear the Lord, you his saints,
>for those who fear him lack nothing.
[10]The lions may grow weak and hungry,
>but those who seek the Lord lack no good thing.
[11]Come, my children, listen to me;
>I will teach you the fear of the Lord.
[12]Whoever of you loves life
>and desires to see many good days,
[13]keep your tongue from evil
>and your lips from speaking lies.
[14]Turn from evil and do good;
>seek peace and pursue it.
[15]The eyes of the Lord are on the righteous
>and his ears are attentive to their cry;
[16]the face of the Lord is against those who do evil,
>to cut off the memory of them from the earth.
[17]The righteous cry out, and the Lord hears them;
>he delivers them from all their troubles.
[18]The Lord is close to the brokenhearted
>and saves those who are crushed in spirit.

¹⁹A righteous man may have many troubles,
        but the Lord delivers him from them all;
²⁰He protects all his bones,
        not one of them will be broken.
²¹Evil will slay the wicked;
        the foes of the righteous will be condemned.
²²The Lord redeems his servants;
        no one will be condemned who takes refuge in him.

— Psalm 34

This magnificent Psalm is full of practical advice for the Christian:

Taste (8). 'Go on, eat it,' I said once to a small two-year old nephew of mine, looking suspiciously at his first strawberry. He did so, and you can imagine the rest. His hand came out for more. The Christian life is like that. 'O make but trial of His love, experience will decide.'

Glorify (3). To glorify is to make glorious; and that is the task of the Christian – '. . . whatever you do, do it all for the glory of God'(1 Corinthians 10:31). Looking at us, and perhaps right through us, people should be able to see a little more clearly what Jesus is like, and begin to want Him for themselves.

Fear (9). 'What does it mean to fear God?' Someone once asked me, as we stood near the sea. 'It's like this,' I said. 'I love the sea, but I have a tremendous respect for it. I regard it with a mixture of affection and awe.' That is how we should regard God, and one result will be that we shall want to 'turn from evil' (14) 'Do not be wise in your own eyes; fear the Lord and shun evil.'(Proverbs 3:7).

Look finally at verse 15. God has a 'telescope' and a 'telephone'. We are never out of his sight, and he gives us a twenty-four hour service. He is always available.

Thought: The Christian life begins as an experiment and ends as an experience.

Prayer

'O how I fear You, living God, with deepest, tenderest fears,...
yet I may love You too, O Lord, almighty as You are, for You have
stooped to ask of me the love of my poor heart'. **Amen**

(27) Sober Confidence

[1] The Lord is my light and my salvation –
  whom shall I fear?
  The Lord is the stronghold of my life –
  of whom shall I be afraid?
[2] When evil men advance against me
  to devour my flesh,
  when my enemies and my foes attack me,
  they will stumble and fall.
[3] Though an army besiege me,
  my heart will not fear;
  though war break out against me,
  even then will I be confident.
[4] One thing I ask of the Lord,
  this is what I seek:
  that I may dwell in the house of the Lord
  all the days of my life,
  to gaze upon the beauty of the Lord
  and to seek him in his temple.
[5] For in the day of trouble
  he will keep me safe in his dwelling;
  he will hide me in the shelter of his tabernacle
  and set me high upon a rock.
[6] Then my head will be exalted
  above the enemies who surround me;
  at his tabernacle will I sacrifice with shouts of joy;
  I will sing and make music to the Lord.
[7] Hear my voice when I call, O Lord;
  be merciful to me and answer me.
[8] My heart says of you, "Seek his face!"
  Your face, Lord, I will seek.
[9] Do not hide your face from me,
  do not turn your servant away in anger;
  you have been my helper.
  Do not reject me or forsake me,
  O God my Saviour.
[10] Though my father and mother forsake me,
  the Lord will receive me.

¹¹ Teach me your way, O Lord;
      lead me in a straight path
      because of my oppressors.
¹² Do not turn me over to the desire of my foes,
      for false witnesses rise up against me,
      breathing out violence.
¹³ I am still confident of this:
      I will see the goodness of the Lord
      in the land of the living.
¹⁴ Wait for the Lord;
      be strong and take heart
      and wait for the Lord.

Psalm 27

This Psalm was probably written by David when the rebellion of Absalom (who was his son) had forced him to leave Jerusalem and seek refuge with his army in the desert. You can read all about it in 2 Samuel 15. But the mood of the psalm meets the need of any who feel themselves to be oppressed (2), overwhelmed (3) and orphaned (10). Throughout the whole of it there rings a note of sober confidence: sober because the problems are too great for our weakness; confidence because they are not too great for God's power. God said to Paul, "My grace is sufficient for you, for my power is made perfect in weakness"(2 Corinthians 12:9).

Notice David's ambition in life (4) – to 'dwell', to 'gaze' and to 'seek him'. Imagine yourself invited to stay in some great castle or palace – isn't that what you would do? You would enter, explore and seek the presence of your host. If you have begun the Christian life, then you have started along this track.

By receiving Christ, we have come to Him, and begun to dwell with Him day by day. As we think about Him and talk to Him, and as we read His word, we find ourselves gazing with wonder at His amazing grace and goodness. This leads us to want to spend more and more time consciously in His presence, sharing our lives with Him and accepting His rule over us.

Thought: The Christian life is one long game of 'Hide' (5) and 'Seek' (8).

Prayer

'Your face, Lord, I will seek. Do not hide Your face from me'. **Amen**

(28) Unfailing Resources

[4]Rejoice in the Lord always. I will say it again: Rejoice! [5]Let your gentleness be evident to all. The Lord is near. [6]Do not be anxious about anything, but in everything, by prayer and petition, with thanksgiving, present your requests to God. [7]And the peace of God, which transcends all understanding, will guard your hearts and your minds in Christ Jesus.

[8]Finally, brothers, whatever is true, whatever is noble, whatever is right, whatever is pure, whatever is lovely, whatever is admirable – if anything is excellent or praiseworthy – think about such things. [9]Whatever you have learned or received or heard from me, or seen in me – put it into practice. And the God of peace will be with you.

[10]I rejoice greatly in the Lord that at last you have renewed your concern for me. Indeed, you have been concerned, but you had no opportunity to show it. [11]I am not saying this because I am in need, for I have learned to be content whatever the circumstances. [12]I know what it is to be in need, and I know what it is to have plenty. I have learned the secret of being content in any and every situation, whether well fed or hungry, whether living in plenty or in want. [13]I can do everything through him who gives me strength.

Philippians 4:4–13

Paul wrote this letter during his two years' imprisonment in Rome (AD 61–63). He was quite well treated, and at this stage was, so to speak, 'on remand'; but he was far from home, his liberty was gone, and he may have guessed already what the final outcome would be. He was executed three or four years later. We might have expected such a strong personality to be writing a letter full of resentment and frustration, or seeking legal advice, or planning an escape. But we look in vain for three things:

Regret *(4). There is nothing to suggest that Paul wished that things had worked out differently, and in the opening chapter he said that he discerned the hand of God in his captivity – 'Now I want you to know, brothers, that what has happened to me has really served to advance the gospel.'(Philippians 1:12). It was one of those 'all things' in which God was working for his good (Romans 8:28).*

Anxiety *(6,7). His own future outlook was grim and bleak, and there was much to concern him among the Christians to whom he was writing, but he was so conscious of the Lord's presence (5), that he was kept in perfect peace. Verse 7 is really saying that to have God's peace about a problem is better than to understand the answer to it.*

Discontent *(11–13). However rough and uncomfortable his situation was, God gave Paul's life the inner lining of His own inexhaustible strength.*

Was Paul exceptional? He doesn't say so; in fact he implies that all Christians should be sharing his experience.

Thought: Jesus taught His followers to think of death, not as a precipice, but as a horizon.

Prayer

Lord, when I cannot rejoice in my circumstances, keep me always rejoicing in You. **Amen**

(29) An Experienced Christian

[1]To the elders among you, I appeal as a fellow elder, a witness of Christ's sufferings and one who also will share in the glory to be revealed: [2]Be shepherds of God's flock that is under your care, serving as overseers – not because you must, but because you are willing, as God wants you to be; not greedy for money, but eager to serve; [3]not lording it over those entrusted to you, but being examples to the flock. [4]And when the Chief Shepherd appears, you will receive the crown of glory that will never fade away.

[5]Young men, in the same way be submissive to those who are older. All of you, clothe yourselves with humility toward one another, because

> "God opposes the proud but gives grace to the humble."

[6]Humble yourselves, therefore, under God's mighty hand, that he may lift you up in due time. [7]Cast all your anxiety on him because he cares for you.

[8]Be self-controlled and alert. Your enemy the devil prowls around like a roaring lion looking for someone to devour. [9]Resist him, standing firm in the faith, because you know that your brothers throughout the world are undergoing the same kind of sufferings.

[10]And the God of all grace, who called you to his eternal glory in Christ, after you have suffered a little while, will himself restore you and make you strong, firm and steadfast. [11]To him be the power for ever and ever. Amen.

1 Peter 5:1-11

This letter was written by Simon Peter, and we see what great progress he has made since those fateful days at the end of the gospel story, and what a great example he was now setting to the younger Christians for whom he was responsible.

Humility (5,6). How proud he had been! But he has now learnt the lesson of humility. In the British Army medal ribbons are never worn on the great coat. They are worn on the tunic, but the great coat covers up all the glory underneath. To 'be clothed with humility' means we don't parade the gifts or achievements we may possess.

Watchful (8). Once before, Peter had slept when he should have watched, but he had learnt that lesson too, and was permanently on his guard against all the wiles and assaults of the enemy.

Courageous (9). What a coward Peter had been! But all that too was changed. The presence of Christ, and the fact that other Christians all over the world were engaged in the same battle, gave him all the strength he needed.

Look at verses 10 and 11. Grace is what God gives us – His love and power flowing towards us day by day; and we, for our part, acknowledge that it all comes from Him and give Him all the credit: 'For every virtue we possess, and every victory won, and every thought of holiness are His alone'.

Thought: We should all be humble, because we have got a great deal to be humble about; and there is none so empty as he who is full of himself.

Prayer

> Lord, help me to live so close to You, who was 'meek and lowly in heart', that some of Your humility may rub off on to me. **Amen**

(30) Into Battle

[1]After the death of Moses the servant of the Lord, the Lord said to Joshua son of Nun, Moses' aide: [2]"Moses my servant is dead. Now then, you and all these people, get ready to cross the Jordan River into the land I am about to give to them – to the Israelites. [3]I will give you every place where you set your foot, as I promised Moses. [4]Your territory will extend from the desert to Lebanon, and from the great river, the Euphrates – all the Hittite country – to the Great Sea on the west. [5]No one will be able to stand up against you all the days of your life. As I was with Moses, so I will be with you; I will never leave you nor forsake you.

[6]"Be strong and courageous, because you will lead these people to inherit the land I swore to their forefathers to give them. [7]Be strong and very courageous. Be careful to obey all the law my servant Moses gave you; do not turn from it to the right or to the left, that you may be successful wherever you go. [8]Do not let this Book of the Law depart from your mouth; meditate on it day and night, so that you may be careful to do everything written in it. Then you will be prosperous and successful. [9]Have I not commanded you? Be strong and courageous. Do not be terrified; do not be discouraged, for the Lord your God will be with you wherever you go."

Joshua 1:1–9

After many years as Moses' deputy, Joshua suddenly found himself in the hot seat, on his own, exposed and vulnerable. It is an experience which, in different ways, could come easily to any of us, when we are plunged into a new position, job or responsibility – or for that matter, when we embark on the Christian life in the first place. How was Joshua to cope? How can we cope? This passage gives us two answers:

Be courageous (6). Yes, but how? What must have helped Joshua, and can help us, was the thought that the God who had stood by Moses would stand by him (5). Our circumstances may change dramatically, our own moods can be very fickle, and even other people unreliable, but the Lord is the 'same yesterday, today and for ever.'(Hebrews 13:8) and we can depend upon Him completely. He called Himself the 'I AM', which means that He is the self-existent One, who is, and who was, and who is to come. So He was and He is and He will be forever the God of Abraham, Isaac and Jacob, of Joshua, of Peter, Paul and John, of all His followers down the ages – and even of you and me.

Be careful (7). Isn't that a contradiction? Can you harness courage and care together? Yes, because what Joshua had to be careful to do was to attend to what God had told him, to heed God's advice and obey God's commands. The 'Book of the Law' (and for us that means the whole Bible) must be constantly **in his mind**, as he ponders and meditates on God's will and purpose; and **on his lips**, as he tries to guide and help those who are under his command or come under his influence.

Thought: Courage is not the absence of danger, but the presence of Christ.

Prayer

Lord, I do not pray for a task equal to my powers, but for powers equal to my task. **Amen**